Poetries

Georges Schehadé

Translated by Austin Carder
Introduction by Adonis

The Song Cave

The Song Cave
www.the-song-cave.com

Earlier versions of the poems on pages 22, 38, and 110 appeared in the 2018 issue of *Big Big Wednesday*

Design and layout by Janet Evans-Scanlon

ISBN: 978-1-7340351-9-3
Library of Congress Control Number: 2021936379

FIRST EDITION

Contents

Introduction

"What is the world if not a place for imagination and astonishment?"

The first question Georges Schehadé's poetic experience poses.

We can nearly see, penetrating to the heart of this experience, human beings move in the core of his alphabet like rainbows or trees or flowers and springs. It is a writing that takes the human's hand in its own, opening for it a marvelous space of images and of relationships between things, between these and the words, between the words and man. I can just now nearly hear the cedars that spread their shade over Gibran's grave ask Georges Schehadé: under what tree did the sun sit down today on its journey toward the sea? And I can nearly hear the answer: it didn't sit down. It was running to meet up with the children playing with the waves in front of the Ras Beirut lighthouse. Georges Schehadé? He writes his poem in an ink mixed with the thirst of legends, the spleen of the trees and the eyelids of the clouds as if his days were paths drawn by the dream on light's notebooks. And here is his poem: fascinating like a breast between the lips of a child suckling with pleasure.

In Schehadé's poem the word is jealous of its sister. Each image is a seduction. The eternal is a butterfly that flutters by between his words and his images. Yes, the reader of his poetry imagines that it is a horizon where he sees the mountain love or adore the water's old age and space giving itself to the wings' childhood.

We do not see streets in Georges Schehadé's poetry, nor factories. We see the sap of cities. Nor do we hear politicians or armies. But we hear the music of the elements, and the rhythms of the imaginary.

Georges Schehadé reads man and his life by writing the legend or the myth and its first light. He speaks of creation by writing the creator himself. He scrutinizes humankind with his piercing gaze, but he writes divinity. And each thing in his language is poetry.

When the water flows through the field one hears the sigh of the plants. Read and listen deeply to the dialogue between Georges Schehadé's poetry and the dead leaves falling or those that grow and wave in the forests of the imaginary. Thus you will see how Georges Schehadé, in each cell of each of his readers, creates wings.

In Georges Schehadé's poetry the universe is winged.

ADONIS
Paris, March 2021
Translated by Pierre Joris

de *Poésies I*

(1938)

Les premières brebis bêlent au marécage
Nous avons sommeillé sous un arbre
La lune montait comme un animal d'orage
Les feuilles du vent brûlaient
Et pour mieux être nous-mêmes avons rêvé
Qu'à chaque tournant de route un homme dormait
Le front irrité de miracles
L'épaule sans ombres du ciel
Et comme nous une bêche près du dormeur
Et ces cris dans la campagne

from *Poetries I*

(1938)

The first sheep bleat in the swamp
We slumbered beneath a tree
The moon charged through leaves
Singed by the wind
And to grow we dreamed
Of a man sleeping
At each bend in the road
His face fraught with wonder
Shoulder stripped of the sky's shadow
Like us a shovel near the sleeper
Crying in the field

Chaque été il y aura donc pour moi
Une nouvelle mélancolie
Et je vous aime comme ce que je vous dis
Pour un cheval blanc comme l'hiver
Les brises dépouillent des rosées
Et les oiseaux meurent des blessures de la mer
Couronnez l'amour qui tient un arc
Une hirondelle a longé le soir
Elle est sans couleur sans force
Cette saison ne passera pas sans un nouvel astre
Son azur est chaud de toutes les nuits

Every summer renews
My melancholy
And I love you
As I've told you
For a white winter horse
Wind uproots the dew
And birds succumb to wounds
Sustained at sea
Crown love drawing a bow
A swallow flew as far as evening
Colorless and without strength
This season will last
Until a new star stirs
Stained a warm blue
By so many nights

Quand je serai au plus loin de la terre
— Ô branches tordues comme nos corps
Rappelle-toi
La patience sereine de mes soupirs
J'avais dit :
Elle est dans les rochers plus fraîche
Que les oiseaux
Mais je sais que tu es pauvre comme les prières

Once I'm far from earth
— O branches bent like
Our bodies
Remember
My silent sighs
I had said:
Atop a boulder
She's lighter than the birds
But I know you are poor as prayer

Ô bien-aimée pleine de pleurs
De plaine en plaine en perdant la vue
Nous nous vivrons dans nos mémoires
Vos mains sont sèches comme les rosiers
Les abeilles sourient à votre calvaire
Ah dans les églises vous revoir
La poitrine rouge comme une pierre
Plus douce que le miel en Jésus
Dont le crachat est un grand brouillard

O tearful beloved
Crossing the plains and losing sight
We'll live in memory
Your hands dry like roses
Bees smile at your path of thorns
Ah in the churches you see
The chest ruddy like a rock
Sweeter than honey in Jesus whose
Spit is a spreading fog

Cette femme qui rêve dans ses habits
Je ne la verrai plus dans les chants
Que la mort la repose
j'épouserai ses mains

— Ce souvenir de Galilée est très petit
Il y avait l'eau et moi tout seul

She dreams in her dress
I won't see her anymore in song
She'll rest in death
                                        I'll marry her hands

— This memory of Galilee is very faint
There was water and me and nothing else

Le vent principal songe des amants
Ni l'enfant de tes paupières
Jeune fille aussi haute que les arbres

À cause d'une peine sans figure
Le vin la tristesse et le soir

The west wind conjures lovers
No child of your eyelids
Girl tall as the trees

A faceless pain to blame
The wine the sadness the night

Cette fleur de la montagne jaunie comme nos larmes
Tu écrivais des choses éternelles ô poussière
De jeune fille
À travers la maison aux caresses des vagues
Et tes yeux ne sont pas dans la rue
Quand les branches seront lassées
De mêler les oiseaux à la terre
Si les lunes sont éphémères comme leurs feuilles tendres
Pour toi la salutation des cloches jusqu'aux perles
Les oliviers qui ont eu des rois
Pour attendre le Temps sous leurs images
Moi je vais mourir de ma patience
— Vous pleurez comme les petits bateaux
Qui coulent sur le visage des mères

This flower on the mountain
Yellowed like our tears
Her dust wrote eternal things
Across the house caressed by waves
Your eyes vacate the street
When branches grow tired
Of blending birds with the earth
If moons melt like their fleeting leaves
The bells beckon and pearls speak
Dethroned olive trees
Wait for Time beneath their reflections
My patience will kill me
— You cry like little boats
Sailing down mothers' faces

Ma mère qui était plus poète que moi
Ma mère écrivait à sa sœur :
Comme une terre la voix est douce

À sa joue une rose à sa joue un livre

My mother was more of a poet than I am
My mother wrote to her sister:
The voice is soft as earth

At her cheek a rose at her cheek a book

Quand tremblera l’automne sur la montagne
Mets à ton cou l’œil des cygnes
Les beautés sont dans le vent et l’heure est noire
Je t’aime on me l’a dit

When autumn sends a shiver
Down the mountain
Place the swan's eye on your neck
Wondrous wind in the dead of night
I love you I've been told

Des anges me couvrent de cette maladie
Mais les belles parties de l'aurore c'est ta bouche

Il y avait toujours une robe de mort pour toi
L'écho battait du tambour tombait du toit

Que tu tournes les yeux du côté de la muraille
Que les printemps réfléchissent dans tes cheveux de longs bois

Angels afflict me with disease
But the height of sunrise is your mouth

There was always a coffin waiting for you
Your quiet corpse caught in cloth

Turn your eyes from the wall
Part the dark woods of your hair to show me spring

La pluie plus douce que des troupeaux ocres
L'eau plus blanche sur ses épaules que le malheur
Je ne sais pas si c'est un signe ou une torture
Cette voix dans mon enfance comme une pomme
Il y a une grande misère dans les villages

Rain softer than ocher herds
Water lighter than a curse on their shoulders
I don't know if this is a sign or torture
This voice in my childhood like an apple
And in the village utter despair

Pauvre Lamartine
J'ai porté tes notes dans un carton
Et nul n'a eu pitié de moi pas même la terre
Celle qui a le sang de chaque fleur

Visage du Poète au bord de l'eau
Tu as délié toute ma vie comme ces barques

Poor Lamartine
I carried your letters in a box
And nobody pitied me not even the dirt
Who holds every flower's blood

Poet's face at the edge of the water
You untied my entire life like these boats

Je vous ai annoncé un grand oiseau de douleur
Au soleil d'or des mois punis
Au soleil des vieilles argiles
Un chant vous déchirera d'une aube à l'autre
Ô belle comme la caresse des platanes
Vous n'avez pas vu la croix des hirondelles
Fougères de la mémoire
La neige salée des feuilles sur les puits

De la cendre sur vos yeux
Si vous avez péché comme les grandes verdures

I pointed to the shadow cast by the giant bird
In the golden sun of punished months
In the old earthen sun
A song will drag you from one morning to the next
And harmonize with rustling sycamores
The swallows' crucifix escaped you
Memory's ferns
The dirty snow of leaves on the well

Ash in your eyes
Since you've sinned like the tall trees

Et je songeais souvent à toi sur l'indésirable mer
Notre désir est triste comme la mort des eaux
L'air a pâli d'un ciel sous les arbres
Et vous êtes encore dans la douleur des jardins
Fermez mes yeux avec la rose de vos genoux
Dans la maison secrète des vivres
Pour tes yeux calices blancs de l'amertume
Les fruits dans la poésie et dans la mer
Nous ne verrons jamais les villes ô lumière
La rose au bord des yeux ô mirage

I saw you in dreams on the barren sea
Desire wanes like dying waves
And the sky's color fled
You're still sealed inside the garden
Close my eyes with the rose of your knees
Among our gathered provisions
White goblets teeming with rage
Where your eyes should be
Sustenance in poetry and in the sea
We'll never reach the cities o light
The rose lining the eyes o mirage

Je m'endormirai volontiers jeune femme
N'éblouissez pas l'oiseau qui me regarde
Les couleurs naissent dans les sommeils
Cette semaine les fleurs sont irrespirables
Et c'est un effort vers ta bouche que je perds
Maintenant que je suis à l'état limpide de pierre
Hors des saisons comme une essence
La bouche mal gardée comme la grille de la route
La nuit jette nos lampes dans les arbres

I'll put myself to bed young lady
Don't blind the bird watching me
Color is born in sleep
This week flowers are unbreathable
And I have lost your mouth
Now that I'm a crystal
An essence outside time
Mouth falling apart like a fence on the roadside
Night throws our lights into the trees

de *Poésies II*

(1948)

Il y a des jardins qui n'ont plus de pays
Et qui sont seuls avec l'eau
Des colombes les traversent bleues et sans nids

Mais la lune est un cristal de bonheur
Et l'enfant se souvient d'un grand désordre clair

from *Poetries II*

(1948)

Some gardens have lost their countries
They're alone with the water
Blue doves with no nests fly over

But the moon is a diamond of delight
And the child recalls a bright disaster

Comme ces lacs qui font très mal
Quand l'automne les couvre et les bleuit
Comme l'eau qui n'a qu'un bruit mille fois le même
Il n'est nul repos pour toi ô ma vie
Les oiseaux volent et s'enchaînent
Chaque sommeil est d'un pays
Et toi dans les feuilles de cette plaine
À l'avant de ton visage tant d'adieu

Like these aching lakes
When fall covers them and turns them blue
Like flowing water an endless echo
Life won't rest
The birds fly in chains
Each sleep has its place
And you in this field
Facing so many farewells

Les arbres qui ne voyagent que par leur bruit
Quand le silence est beau de mille oiseaux ensemble
Sont les compagnons vermeils de la vie
Ô poussière savoureuse des hommes

Les saisons passent mais peuvent les revoir
Suivre le soleil à la limite des distances
Puis — comme les anges qui touchent la pierre
Abandonnés aux terres du soir

Et ceux-là qui rêvent sous leurs feuillages
Quand l'oiseau est mûr et laisse ses rayons
Comprendront à cause des grands nuages
Plusieurs fois la mort et plusieurs fois la mer

Trees travel only by sound
The sublime silence of a thousand birds
Life's crimson companions
O splendid human dust

Seasons pass but could come back
Follow the sun to the horizon's edge
Then — like angels touching stone
Abandoned in the dirt at dusk

And those dreaming under their leaves
When the bird learns to fly
Seeing in the colossal clouds
Death over and over the sea over again

À Charles Lucet.

Ils ne savent pas qu'ils ne vont plus revoir
Les vergers d'exil et les plages familières
Les étoiles qui voyagent avec des jambes de sel
Quand la nuit est triste de plusieurs beautés

Ils oublient qu'ils ne vont plus entendre
Le vent de la grille et le chien des images
L'eau qui dort sur la couleur des pierres
La nuit avec des violons de pluie

Tant de magie pour rien
Si ce n'était ce souvenir d'un autre monde
Avec des oiseaux de chair dans la prairie
Avec des montagnes comme des granges
Ô mon enfance ô ma folie

for Charles Lucet.

They don't know
This is their last time seeing
Exiled orchards and familiar shores
Stars swim with arms of salt
As beauty saddens the night

They forget
This is their last time hearing
Wind in the garden and the barking image
Water resting on red rocks
Night with violins of rain

All this magic for nothing
If this wasn't the memory of another world
Fleshly birds in the meadow
Mountains pointed like barns
O my childhood o my madness

Les rivières et les roses des batailles
Drapeau doux bercé par le fer

Des plaines sans pays brillaient
Puis la neige méchante et blanche

Les fourmis mangeaient la robe des merveilles
Combien lentes étaient les années

Quand tu portais tablier d'écolier
Quand tu dormais chaque nuit sur ton enfance

Rivers and roses of battle
Soft flag cradled by iron

Stateless plains glimmered
Then the mean white snow

The ants ate the dazzling dress
How slowly the years passed

When you wore a school uniform
When you slept each night on your childhood

Un violon aveugle pleurait pour nous
Une fontaine de pierre
L'hiver la saison sans figure
Quand les raisins sont noirs

A blind violin mourned us
A stone fountain
Winter the faceless season
When grapes are black

Je me déciderai dans un jardin de pommes
Dans cette eau de la campagne
Aux pas immaculés
Et pour toi amie des saules de la mort
Les colombes qui volent sans air
L'absence plus longue que les années

I'll cheer up in an apple garden
In this country water
With immaculate steps
And for you
Friend of lifeless willows
Doves flying without air
Absence longer than the years

de *Poésies III*

(1949)

À Pierre Robin.

Quand l'oiseau se déchire avec son chant
Les feuilles incertaines de leur mélancolie
Parfois cessent leur plainte
L'air au loin finit et ne veut plus entendre
Nous passons alors avec nos chiens de dimanche
Sur le ciel et dans le verger
Et pour l'exil de nos images
Nous donnons une ombre à chaque enfant du soir

from *Poetries III*

(1949)

for Pierre Robin

When the bird rends itself with song
Leaves might grow silent
Doubting their melancholy
In the distance the tune dies
No longer willing to listen
So we walk our Sunday dogs
Across the sky and through the orchard
And exile our reflections
Giving a shadow to each of evening's children

De l'automne jauni qui tremble dans le bois dételé
Il demeure une étrange mélancolie
Comme ces chaînes qui ne sont ni pour le corps ni pour l'âme

Ô saison les puits n'ont pas encore déserté votre grâce
Ce soir nous avançons dans vos feuilles qui passent
Près d'une cascade de triste folie

Et voici dans un nuage de grande transparence
L'étoile comme une étincelle de faim

Yellow autumn trembling on endless trees
Confirms a strange sorrow like these chains
Binding neither body nor soul

O autumn the wells keep your grace
Tonight we greet your fading leaves
Near a dark cascade of madness

And in this crystal-clear cloud
The star like a spark of hunger

Celui qui pense et ne parle pas
Un cheval l'entraîne vers la Bible

Un bâton ne lui fait pas peur
Car l'esprit ne l'a point quitté

Celui qui rêve se mélange à l'air

He who thinks and doesn't speak
Follows a horse toward the Bible

No weapon can frighten him
Since his spirit remains intact

He who dreams dissolves into air

Un corbeau parle sur la montagne
Ma mère en son pays se souvenait

Quelle pourriture ou quelle nacre
Si jamais je reviens ô fontaine
Si l'ombre d'un arbre me conserve son jour

A raven speaks on the mountain
My mother remembers her homeland

So rotten and so rich
If I never return
O fountain
If the shadow of a tree
Retains the day for me

de *Poésies IV:* *Si tu rencontres un ramier*

(1951)

Dans le sommeil quelquefois
Des graines éveillent des ombres
Il vient des enfants avec leurs mondes
Légers comme des ossements de fleurs
Alors dans un pays lointain si proche par le chagrin de l'âme
Pour rejoindre le pavot des paupières innocentes
Les corps da la nuit deviennent la mer

from *Poetries IV:*
If you come across a ring-dove

(1951)

Sometimes in sleep
Seeds awaken shadows
Children bring their worlds
Weightless as the bones of flowers
In a distant land that grief brings near
Night's body becomes the sea
To meet innocent eyelids
Framing the poppy

Pour retrouver le corps et l'âme de l'enfance
Dans une chambre douce allumée de voleurs
Mes mains sont légères lorsque je pense

Un âne venait de la patrie des tableaux
Les bruits alors n'avaient pas de mémoire

C'est ainsi que sont les objets de la grâce
L'oiseau de sucre avec sa romance et le ciel bleu de rien

To find the essence of childhood
In a room lit softly by thieves
My hands rise as soon as I think

A donkey emerged from a landscape
Sound had no memory

All of these objects of grace
The arctic bird with its ballad and the useless blue of the sky

Dans l'histoire des songes dans les veillées du jour
Ce sont les princes de l'ordre
L'absence les protège et les lie
Comme l'ombre à la soie des voyages
De vieux jardins ont ravi leur patience
Ils reviendront quand cessera la distance
— L'herbe les couvre de mirabelles

The history of dreams
The twilight hours
Are keeping order
Absence protects and connects them
Shadow wrapped in rippling silk
Abandoned gardens revoke their patience
They'll return when distance ends
— The grass draping them in plums

La rose qu'on endort dans un tablier
Respire encore pour le temps de son âme
— Qui habite les songes ne meurt jamais
Comme moi et l'eau au fond de l'eau
Sur un lac je me penche
Je n'ai plus de bruits
Mais les fers vieillis d'une image

The rose we tuck into an apron
Inhales and exhales its soul
— Whoever lives in dreams never dies
Like me and the bottom of the lake
I lean over the water
There's no noise
Except the old clang of reflection

Pour Saint-John Perse.

Donnez-lui la racine du laurier
Et non ces fleurs d'un jour qui font la cendre

Poète de la neige et du sablier
Quand ce qui est blanc est l'honneur de la mort

For Saint-John Perse.

Give him the root of the laurel
And not a day's flowers turning to ash

Poet of snow and the hourglass
When what's white is the honor of death

de *Poésies V*

(1972)

La taille des jeunes filles flottait dans le vent
L'oiseau à l'œil de perle ne laissait pas de trace
C'était l'époque des anges Oh je me souviens
La Terre heureuse avait le jour et la nuit pour enfants
L'absence gardait le sourire et la parole
Tout brillait de rien : l'herbe et la lampe
À l'exception d'un cheval cabré qui montait la garde
Et criait vers moi :
Une fois n'est pas coutume sauf pour la mort
Oh je me souviens

from *Poetries V*

(1972)

Girls fluttered in the wind
The pearly-eyed bird left no trace
It was the age of angels Oh I remember
Day and night were Earth's offspring
Absence saved a smile and speech
Everything glowed: the grass and the lamp
But not the horse standing guard
Who shouted at me:
Just once can't hurt except when it comes to death
Oh I remember

La nuit parfois les Saints me visitent
Ils passent à travers les vitres comme on voit dehors les plantes
Et je les reconnais à leurs têtes de marionnettes
Car ils aiment jouer avec mon cœur
Ils font un pas dans la maison
Un autre vers un théâtre de pourpre
Puis redeviennent ce qu'ils sont
C'est-à-dire de beauté invisible
— Seul témoin du miracle
Une poupée oubliée par mégarde
Les yeux fermés comme personne devant les songes

Some nights Saints visit me
They pass through windowpanes
The way we see plants outside
And I know them by their puppet-heads
Since they like playing with my heart
They step into the house
And move toward a purple stage
Before reverting to their true selves
By which I mean unseen beauty
— Only testament to this miracle
A forgotten doll
Eyes closed like any dreamer

Dans l'espace vide et plein comme un anneau
Les grilles de la nuit s'ouvrent sur la mort ou les songes
Cette nuit dans la plaine il y a la Mésopotamie et ses fenêtres
La rose se chauffe à la lampe comme une sœur
Oh regarde
Un voilier à tête de lion jette l'ancre
Et toujours sur la plage
Les grandes rides blanches de la mer

In a space empty and full like a ring
The gates of night open on death or dreams
Mesopotamia and its windows glow tonight
The rose warms herself under the lamp like a nun
Oh look
A boat with a lion figurehead is dropping anchor
And on the beach
The sea's long white wrinkles

Ceux-là qui veillent très tard la nuit
Dans l'absolution profonde des ténèbres
Loin des lampes chaudes aux yeux
Dans l'air nu
Sont les voyageurs de l'avenir
Et les étoiles le savent bien qui s'arrêtent à leurs fenêtres
Laissant des échelles brillantes
À l'aube quand les chasseurs font des trous
Dans le silence des campagnes

Those who stay up late into the night
In the absolving dark
Warm eyes far from light
In the naked air
Are travelers from the future
The stars know who stops at their windows
Who leaves shimmering ladders
At dawn when hunters dig
In the silence of open fields

Ma mère allumait les lampes pour éloigner les ombres de nous
Elle comptait notre âge sur les doigts quand l'horloge frappait ses coups
Ma mère parlait du temps qui passe en souriant
— Et les hommes qui la suivaient étaient ses anges

Maintenant que la lune est morte Où êtes-vous merveilleuses pensées
Amour aux dents de dragées
Enfance qui pleurez sur mes joues

My mother lit lamps to chase the shadows from us
She counted our ages on her fingers as the clock struck
My mother smiled as she spoke of the past
— The men who followed her were her angels

Now that the moon is dead Where are you wondrous thoughts
Love with sugar-coated teeth
Childhood crying on my cheeks

Elle se levait la nuit pour regarder le Christ
Elle touchait le bronze de sa plaie pour guérir
Et son corps tremblait comme du jasmin

— J'aime dans l'obscurité la profondeur de votre ombre
Vous pleurez si doucement qu'en vous touchant on meurt
Et nul n'a les Vierges de vos lèvres
Que votre image

She got up in the middle of the night to look at Christ
She touched his bronze wound to heal herself
And her body trembled like jasmine

— I love the depth of your shadow in the dark
You cry so softly that if anyone touched you they would die
And the Virgins of your lips belong to no one
Except your reflection

Si jamais tu reviens en terre natale
À pas lents comme un cheval dont le soir accroît la fatigue
Oh va dans ce jardin
Retrouver la rose méconnaissable
Le chrysanthème à la crinière de lion
— D'immenses araignées volent avec des papillons
Comme dans les fièvres de l'enfance
Souris ou pleure mais ne crains rien
C'est l'ombre qui remue avant d'être nuit claire

If you ever return to your native land
Slow steps like a horse at the end of the day
Come to this garden
Locate the unknowable rose
The chrysanthemum with a lion's mane
— Giant spiders soaring with butterflies
Like in a fever dream of childhood
Smile or cry but don't be afraid
The shadow stirs
Then turns to luminous night

Dans l'automne rouge et jaune comme un tamis à travers les arbres
Et la fumée d'un zéphyr
Un corbeau à béquilles prédit des malheurs

Songeant à la jeune fille qui passe dans le bois
Pareille à une fable
Je crie : Ô amour accorde-lui longue vie

Mais l'écho qui vient de loin et qui plie
Perdant des mots reprend :
Amour amour sans vie

Comme un jeu de cartes

Autumn like a red and yellow net cast over the trees
The smoke of a gentle breeze
A limping crow portends disaster

Dreaming of the girl wandering in the woods
Like in a fairytale
I shout: O love grant her long life

But the echo returns and twists
Losing my words it answers:
Love love has lost its life

In a card game

Quand la tristesse et la joie de la mer
Se mélangent séparément — sur la plage au déclin du jour
Elle dit : Si la mélancolie me surprenait
Je m'étendrais sur le sable nain
Pour être nue et pour mourir
Et moi je pensais que la mort
C'est d'abord les yeux fermés
Une nuit blanche dans les fleurs
Et la prière

Puis quatre cierges au souffle d'or

When the sea's sadness and joy
Blend apart on the shore at sunset
She says: If melancholy surprised me
I'd stretch myself out on the grains of sand
Naked and ready to die
And I'd think death
Is first of all closed eyes
A white night drenched in flowers
And prayer

Then four candles on the altar
In a golden breath

Dans la cage d'un oiseau il y a un jardin de tristesse
Et toute la mélancolie d'une maison

Les ailes sont des feuilles vertes
Dans le jour frugal et cassé
Comme des miettes

Je me souviens pauvre écolier
À la fenêtre

In a birdcage there's a garden of sadness
And all the melancholy of a house

Wings are green leaves
In the day cheap and crushed
Like crumbs

I remember poor schoolboy
At the window

Quand il fait un peu de lune
Sur le lit de ta chambre
Rejoins sur une carte
L'immensité comme une fille

En terre d'Amazonie
Sur une feuille fraîche
Écris ceci :
L'Europe est une rose

Dans les villes de pierres
Où les corps souffrent et chantent
Rien n'est plus chaste
Que la géographie

When there's a sliver of moon
On your bed
Look for immensity
On the map
Like a little girl

In the Amazon
On a crisp leaf
Write this:
Europe is a rose

In cities of stone
Where bodies suffer and sing
Nothing is more chaste
Than geography

Ni l'espérance ni la fortune
Mais la petite fleur desséchée dans un livre
Dont il reste seulement la cendre d'amour

— Comment mourir
Quand on peut encore rêver

Neither hope nor luck
But the little dried flower in a book
Of which only love's ashes remain

— How to die
When dreaming is still possible

Le bruit d'un coquillage n'est pas celui de la mer
Ni le voyage du vent
Mais le chant et la tombe d'un sommeil

Comme les épines sont les pleurs de la rose dans le matin
Et le lys le souvenir des rois
Ah tant de mélancolie sur les choses

A seashell doesn't sound like the ocean
Or the wind blowing
It sounds like the song and tomb of sleep

The rose's tears are like thorns in the morning
And the lily the memory of monarchs
So much melancholy dwells in things

de *Poésies VI:* *Le Nageur d'un seul amour*

(1985)

Elle marchait dans un verger
De douces syllabes tombaient des arbres
L'air n'avait plus de couleur

C'est la naissance du soir
La première fraîcheur des nids
Rêvait un peu la jeune fille
En regardant autour d'elle

Maintenant la nuit se répète à l'infini
Les arbres se cachent dans leurs feuilles
Et le silence arrive de loin

from *Poetries VI: Lone love's swimmer*

(1985)

She walked through an orchard
Of soft fallen syllables
The air had lost its color

Birth of evening
The first chill of nests
Dreamed the young girl
Looking around

Eternal return of night
Trees hide in their leaves
And silence approaches from afar

Hommage à Fra Angelico.

Ma mère appelait les anges par leurs prénoms :
Gabriel aux doigts de violon
Aux ailes de coquillages
Et Marie, Marie seule dans la maison
Les yeux baissés sur son visage
Tout ça dans une chambre où il n'y a rien
Peut-être et seulement
Le pain et l'eau pour les louanges

Homage to Fra Angelico.

My mother called the angels by their names:
Gabriel with violin fingers
With seashell wings
And Mary, Mary alone in the house
Looking down
On a room containing nothing
Maybe and only
Bread and water for the blessings

Comme un enfant d'autrefois dont le cri se perd
Dans un verger de pommes blanches
Quand la lune couvre tout de son amour
Je revois dans un miroir désert
Mes souvenirs avec des cannes blanches
Et je ne sais pas qui d'eux ou bien de moi
Est le plus à plaindre
Tellement les années sont cruelles

Lune légère ô miroir d'absence

Like a child from the past whose voice drowns
In an orchard of white apples
When the tender moon covers everything
I glimpse in an empty mirror
My memories with white canes
And I don't know if I should feel more sorry
For them or for myself
How cruel the years have been

Weightless moon o mirror of absence

Dans l'église du village à l'approche de la nuit
Les prières sortent de leurs cachettes
Un ange enfant change de mur

L'encens prête sa couverture d'ombre
À des Mages endormis
Les lys à leurs pieds paraissent obscurs

Et plus loin dans un ciel de bougies
Les icônes voyagent

In the village church at dusk
Prayers leave their niches
An angel changes walls

Incense shelters sleeping wise men
With its shadow
Lilies barely visible at their feet

And across the candlelit sky
Icons fly

Avant le sommeil
Les sœurs de ma mère parlaient si bas
Que tout devenait de l'ombre
Les visages et les voix
Jusqu'à l'horloge dans sa cage
Qui n'avait plus de chant
Une allumette alors brillait
Et l'on pouvait entrevoir
Mes tantes agenouillées
Dans une goutte d'or

Before bed
My mother's sisters spoke so softly
That everything became shadow
Faces and voices
Even the clock in its cage
With no song left
A match flickered
And you could glimpse
My kneeling aunts
In a drop of gold

Les Saintes Femmes.

Au pied de la Croix
Quand l'ombre éclaire les étoiles du ciel
Femmes angéliques et noires
Percez votre cœur de votre doigt

The Holy Women.

At the foot of the cross
When shadows ignite the stars
Women angelic and dark
Pierce your heart with your finger

Ce n'est pas des mots pour rien ce poème
Ce n'est pas un chant pour personne cette mélancolie
Voici l'automne et ses froides étoiles
Il reste assez de vent pour s'enfuir
L'oiseau d'Afrique demande l'heure
Mais la mer est loin comme un voyage
Et les pays se perdent dans les pays
— Écoute à travers les ramures
Le bruit doré d'un arbre qui meurt

This poem
Not words for nothing
This sorrow
Not a song for no one
Autumn has arrived with its cold stars
There's still enough wind to escape
The African bird asks the time
But the sea is a journey away
And countries fade into countries
— Listen through the branches
For the golden sound of a dying tree

Sur cette plage abandonnée
Elle ne venait que pour s'en aller
Comme les vagues de la mer
Aujourd'hui le temps qui passe ajoute à sa beauté
L'ombre et le souvenir
— Que disait-elle tout bas
Quand elle mêlait les mots avec ses mains

Pauvre que j'étais
J'allais ainsi dans mes pensées
À la rencontre d'une absence
Tandis qu'à l'horizon soulevés par la brume
De grands arbres à mi-voix parlaient aux saisons

On this empty beach
She comes only to leave again
Like waves
Today passing time adds to her beauty
Shadow and memory
— What was she whispering
As she blended words with her hands

Poor thing that I was
I went into my thoughts
To find absence
While on the horizon lifted by mist
Tall trees spoke to the seasons in hushed tones

Stèle pour Nadia T. . .

Elle a quitté la main de ses amis
Pour un jardin tout bleu fermé
Où l'oiseau s'envole avec son nid

Yeux noirs cheveux noirs
Et maintenant toutes les beautés de l'ombre
Sur ses épaules

Memorial for Nadia T. . .

She slipped from her friends' hand
Into a garden locked in blue
Where the bird carries off its nest

Black eyes black hair
And all the shadow's beauty
Now on her shoulders

Au lever du jour
Les pigeons articulaient leurs pas
Dans la cour

La pluie tombait
Semant ses graines d'eau
Sur les pavés

At daybreak
Pigeons pronounced their steps
In the courtyard

Rain fell
Sowing its seeds
Across the stones

Elle était plus vieille que le temps
Avec des mains de grande transparence
Et dans les yeux la tristesse du printemps

On l'a couchée sous le sable
Il y avait un peu de vent dans les arbres
Il n'y avait plus rien

Reste le souvenir de sa voix
Depuis qu'elle est dans ce pays lointain
Où toutes les femmes se ressemblent

She was older than time
With transparent hands
In her eyes the sadness of spring

We laid her on the sand
There was a breeze in the branches
Nothing else

Beside the memory of her voice
Since she had been in that distant land
Where all women look alike

Quand les yeux se perdent dans le sommeil
Comme au fond d'un puits les visages
Il vient un songe avec ses paysages
Sur le dormeur de la nuit
Et c'est dans un ciel noir fuyant ses étoiles
Une fenêtre à l'aurore
Avec une tête penchée de femme
Et qui demeure dans le songe une énigme

When eyes vanish in sleep
Like faces at the bottom of a well
A dream pours its landscapes
Over the night's sleeper
A dark sky flees its stars

In a window at dawn
A woman bows her head
Still unknown in the dream

Translator's Note

"[His] poems are something like extremely precise clocks that never give the right hour; perhaps they give a different one, outside of time."

—OCTAVIO PAZ

The poems Georges Schehadé wrote throughout the almost half-century between 1938 and 1985 form a translucent chain in his collection *Les Poésies*. The (non-)title of the volume—meant to stand as the definitive embodiment of the author's poetic output—points to the real illusion of abstract purity with which they enchant the reader. Schehadé might have called his poetic lifework *Les Poèmes* [The Poems] or *Poésie* [Poetry], but instead he chose an oddly synthetic term in which the antinomies of poetry as a mode and the poem as its incarnation dissolve into each other. Each poem holds all of poetry, all of history: "Dreams of the past precede the dawn of the future—the present is the point at which the truth can be penetrated, the single fulcrum on which everything hinges."*

The voice of *Les Poésies* suggests a lullaby or an enigmatic fairytale told before bed. Its tone is one of self-sufficient prayer—a pronouncement

* Patrick Zapien, "A Little History of Painting" *Caesura* Issue 0

rather than a plea—addressed to no one in particular and to anyone. These weathered songs key into the language of music, not by approximating its effects but by innervating sparks of meaning that flash forth. Schehadé's broken-off parables convulse with the dual beauty of both hymn and elegy. They revel and mourn in the same breath. The poetries sustain an elevated, buoyant tension before gently falling in the last line, in the last light. These are refined objects, but not precious or overwrought. Each poem is a crystal conspicuously lacking ornament.

Schehadé considered the artist's role in the passive terms of watching over the birth of his poems. He felt himself to be the means by which they realized themselves. He did not write so much as transcribe, and he greeted each poem with surprise. It is almost a theory of translation, and his approach gave me courage in negotiating the challenges of my own task—one of more explicit mediation. Schehadé's spirit endows a shortcut to the sympathetic resonance necessary for translation. The poet preceded me in subjecting himself to the matter at hand, already having first allowed this language to speak.

*

Though he was born in Egypt and spent most of his life in Lebanon, Schehadé considered himself a French poet—a poet of the French language. It was that tradition which seeded his poems; it was French poetry (or *modern* poetry tout court) into which he wrote. An exception to the relative neglect of Schehadé's work is Jean-Pierre Richard's *Onze études sur la poésie moderne* (1973), in which he considers Schehadé among the canonical figures of twentieth century French poetry including Pierre Reverdy, René Char, Paul Éluard, Francis Ponge, and Yves Bonnefoy.

Surrealism is the school that shaped Schehadé's vision. His formative influences were Rimbaud, Lautréamont, Jules Supervielle, Éluard, Max Jacob, and Saint-John Perse. Introduced by Éluard to André Breton's surrealist group when visiting Paris in 1948, Schehadé forged lasting friendships with many of its members. Walter Benjamin wrote that the Surrealists exchange "the play of human features for the face of an alarm clock that in each minute rings for sixty seconds."* Poetry's forms appeared exhausted and its *raison d'être* obscured. Yet this was not merely a problem of art but also one of life—the life that art objectifies. The historical crisis of subjectivity registered by the Surrealists makes itself felt in Schehadé's poetry in ways that are gentler but no less stark. Though Schehadé's imagery and atmosphere of ambivalence bind him to Surrealism, his touch diverges from those of his comrades in the particularity of its sensual aspect. As Breton indelibly put it, "If you asked me what Georges Schehadé's secret is, I'd answer in the old language of falconry—that he knows like no one else how to get at the *lure*."†

Intimations of *la vie antérieure* suffuse an evocative arsenal of distant gardens, forests, birds, fountains, and shadows. These images surge up cyclically, feeling both familiar and strange each time they appear. Despite how few of them there are, Schehadé's motifs achieve an astonishing breadth in their graceful unfolding. Richard describes the peculiarity of their effect as follows: "all of this will be felt by the soul as a dwelling upon, and as an absence."‡ Utopia flashes up in its withdrawal past a steadily receding horizon; it appears as an innocence and a being-at-home that never quite *was*. What distinguishes these poems from simple nostalgia? Richard goes on to say that Schehadé's "obsessions constitute a vast imaginary constellation of absence, an absence that envelops and points—with melancholy—toward true presence."

The arresting line "Some gardens have lost their countries" speaks to the realm of remembrance where damaged experience survives in trans-

---

* Walter Benjamin, "Surrealism" (1929), translated by Edmund Jephcott

† Quoted in Thierry Fabre, "Georges Schehadé, poète des deux rives" (2000), my translation

‡ Jean-Pierre Richard, *Onze études sur la poésie moderne* (1973), my translation

figured form. We might consider it emblematic of Schehadé's œuvre. His poems are distinct artifacts of what Benjamin called the "organization of pessimism" that defined surrealist practice. They organize it paradoxically with the pull of a nostalgia that subsumes its opposite. This world of static animation condenses into an after-image contorted by longing. In place of odes to the homeland, unanswerable songs of homesickness reach our ears. Herein lies the *critical* element of Schehadé's poetry, that which guards it against lapsing into mere consolation. Schehadé's fleeting reverie is the index of the nightmare from which the poem hides its face and about which it has nothing to "say." He was writing, after all, during the darkest period of modern history and lived his final years in the shadow of the Lebanese Civil War. If the poem is, as Theodor W. Adorno suggested, "a philosophical sundial telling the time of history," we must ask ourselves how much we remain the contemporaries of a barbaric twentieth century.* Whatever "true presence" might mean, Schehadé's constellation of absence will resonate as long as it eludes us.

*

Schehadé's friend Octavio Paz wrote that he "did not doubt, or cross out, or correct: his poems fell on the page like the ripe fruits of an invisible tree."† His translator, however, has constantly doubted, crossed out, and corrected. That which mysteriously and effortlessly made its way through Schehadé struggled to be born in English, ample and shimmering. Some of the words for which I first reached, some of the words Schehadé might have used had he written in English, were not always able to deliver on the poem's promise. Correspondence to the French does not mean that any given word would find its place within an Eng-

* Theodor W. Adorno, "Lyric Poetry and Society" (1957), translated by Shierry Weber Nicholsen

† Octavio Paz, "Georges Schehadé" (1989), translated by Gabriel Almeida

lish poem, which is what the translation had to become. Schehadé's unit is an image conscious of the breath in which it lives. The particular words that comprise it are not incidental, nor are they inviolable. The model of the French sound-form asks to be reenacted from within, its contours followed and not merely repeated. Strict faithfulness would have meant a greater betrayal, and so a loyalty to the salient features of these *Poetries* and the physiognomy of their effect means that they have undergone a marked change. They are no longer themselves; they may continue becoming more themselves for this reason.

The architecture of remembering is at stake in this movement, and the weaving of Schehadé's memory eclipses whatever lived experience might lie at its root. These are memories so sharply summoned that they turn back upon themselves and become direct experience again—or for the first time—as *remembrance*. It is not about what really happened or how it really was; this remembrance of the past is how the poem relates to its own present. The relation occurs in and as its language, which is no transparent medium. Another remembrance takes place in my versions, and history enlists itself in service of more life. Schehadé's images free dreams from sleep. They are very near; you meet them face-to-face. And yet, they slip through your fingers as soon as you try to pin them down. Translating them has meant letting them slip through mine. The flood of remembrance, inundating the prehistory and afterlife of the poem, unites my action with its occasion and blends Poetry with these poems.

AUSTIN CARDER

GEORGES SCHEHADÉ was born in Alexandria, Egypt on November 2, 1905 to a French-speaking Greek Orthodox family from Lebanon. Following financial and medical difficulties, the family returned to Lebanon in 1920, settling in the Achrafieh district of Beirut. Schehadé studied business and law, eventually securing a job at the Lebanese Ministry of Justice. In 1928, Schehadé financed the publication of his first collection of poems, *Étincelles*—a work he subsequently disowned and never republished. In 1930, he became the administrative assistant of the influential French literary critic and professor, Gabriel Bounoure. Bounoure would go on to establish Beirut's *École Supérieure des Lettres* and name Schehadé its first general secretary. Bounoure proved decisive to Schehadé's literary career, introducing him to a reading public in France in 1930 by facilitating the publication of his poems in the magazine *Commerce*, edited by Paul Valéry, Léon-Paul Fargue, and Valery Larbaud.

On his first trip to Europe in 1933, Schehadé befriended the poets Jules Supervielle, Max Jacob, and Saint-John Perse, whose work he had long admired and who went on to champion his writing in Paris. Schehadé's first book of poems, *Poésies (I),* appeared in 1938 with Guy Lévis Mano's renowned GLM artisan publishing house. It was this book which first caught the attention of both Octavio Paz and Paul Éluard. GLM printed fine editions of Schehadé's poetry until the preeminent French publisher Gallimard gathered *Poésies I, II, III,* and *IV* in the 1952 *Les Poésies.* In 1951, Schehadé married Brigitte Collerais, with whom he had one son, Élie-Philippe.

Schehadé remained in Lebanon for the duration of the Second World War and then returned to Paris in 1946 and '48. On his third trip, Éluard introduced him to leading figures of the Parisian avant-garde, including André Breton and the Surrealist group, whose influence on Schehadé's work preceded their meeting and is evident throughout his literary production. However, Schehadé does not primarily owe his modest reputation to his poetry. Where he is known, he is known as a dramatist.

In 1951, Schehadé premiered his first play, *Monsieur Bob'le* (directed by Georges Vitaly) in Paris at the Théâtre de la Huchette. It provoked a strong condemnation by theater critics who moved to shut down its production. Writers including Breton, Paz, René Char, Philippe Jaccottet, and Henri Michaux rushed to its defense and prevailed, ensuring its run for 47 performances. Schehadé's subsequent plays would be directed by Jean-Louis Barrault. His best-known work, *Histoire de Vasco* (1956), was translated into 25 languages—including a freely-rendered English libretto by Ted Hughes. This remains the only piece of Schehadé's work to appear in English. Another play, *L'Émigré de Brisbane,* entered the repertory of the Comédie-Française in 1967. In 1958, Schehadé wrote the screenplay for a film called *Goha* starring Omar Sharif, which won the International Critics Prize at the Cannes Film Festival.

Schehadé published *Poésies V* in 1972. He decided to remain in Beirut after the Lebanese Civil War began in 1975, but three years later, following the death of his mother, he relocated to Paris with his wife and son for the remainder of his life. He published a final book of poetry, *Poésies VI*, in 1985, containing poems written over the previous 20 years. In 1986, the Académie Française selected him as the inaugural winner of the prestigious Grand Prix de la Francophonie. Another group of poems, *Poésies VII*, was posthumously brought out by the Lebanese publishing house Dar An-Nahar in 1998. Georges Schehadé died in 1989 in Paris, where he is buried.

Austin Carder is a writer and translator based in Philadelphia. He received his BA in English at Yale and is a PhD candidate in the department of Comparative Literature at Brown. He is also an Editor at *Caesura* (caesuramag.org).

Acknowledgments

I would like to thank the following people without whom this translation would not have been possible: Selen Uman, whose voice cradled these poems in many iterations of themselves. Peter Cole taught me the art of translation and ensured the embodiment of this book's music. Gwen Harper has read these pieces with care over the course of their life in my English. Cole Swensen advised on the presentation of this text and lent her ear to its movements. Constance Sherak helped me grasp the texture and tone of the French. Charlotte Mandell shared Schehadé with the world of readers at *Metambesen*. Molly Schaeffer published earlier versions of three poems in *Big Big Wednesday*. Irakli Qolbaia tended to the weft and warp of the whole. Thank you to Mia Ruf for throwing a careful kick of the eye at this book in the eleventh hour; ça m'a fait plaisir. Forrest Gander, Mónica de la Torre, Charles Bernstein, Elias Muhanna, Robyn Creswell, and Etel Adnan all provided encouragement and guidance at key moments in this project's life.

Pierre Joris wove the legendary Adonis into this book, and Adonis has generously penned a vital tribute to Schehadé's art. Last but not least, the visionaries Ben Estes and Alan Felsenthal's belief in these poems ensured their safe passage into your hands.

This translation seeks to honor and extend the poetic achievement of Georges Schehadé. I regret that he cannot read what we have produced together. I thank him for having offered—and for offering anew—these poetries to the world.

A.C.

OTHER TITLES FROM THE SONG CAVE:

1. *A Dark Dreambox of Another Kind* by **Alfred Starr Hamilton**
2. *My Enemies* by **Jane Gregory**
3. *Rude Woods* by **Nate Klug**
4. *Georges Braque and Others* by **Trevor Winkfield**
5. *The Living Method* by **Sara Nicholson**
6. *Splash State* by **Todd Colby**
7. *Essay Stanzas* by **Thomas Meyer**
8. *Illustrated Games of Patience* by **Ben Estes**
9. *Dark Green* by **Emily Hunt**
10. *Honest James* by **Christian Schlegel**
11. *M* by **Hannah Brooks-Motl**
12. *What the Lyric Is* by **Sara Nicholson**
13. *The Hermit* by **Lucy Ives**
14. *The Orchid Stories* by **Kenward Elmslie**
15. *Do Not Be a Gentleman When You Say Goodnight* by **Mitch Sisskind**
16. *HAIRDO* by **Rachel B. Glaser**
17. *Motor Maids across the Continent* by **Ron Padgett**
18. *Songs for Schizoid Siblings* by **Lionel Ziprin**
19. *Professionals of Hope*, The Selected Writings of **Subcomandante Marcos**
20. *Fort Not* by **Emily Skillings**
21. *Riddles, Etc.* by **Geoffrey Hilsabeck**

22. *CHARAS: The Improbable Dome Builders*, by **Syeus Mottel** (Co-published with Pioneer Works)

23. *YEAH NO* by **Jane Gregory**

24. *Nioque of the Early-Spring* by **Francis Ponge**

25. *Smudgy and Lossy* by **John Myers**

26. *The Desert* by **Brandon Shimoda**

27. *Scardanelli* by **Friederike Mayröcker**

28. *The Alley of Fireflies and Other Stories* by **Raymond Roussel**

29. *CHANGES: Notes on Choreography* by **Merce Cunningham** (Co-published with the Merce Cunningham Trust)

30. *My Mother Laughs* by **Chantal Akerman**

31. *Earth* by **Hannah Brooks-Motl**

32. *Everything and Other Poems* by **Charles North**

33. *Paper Bells* by **Phan Nhiên Hạo**

34. *Photographs: Together & Alone* by **Karlheinz Weinberger**

35. *A Better Place Is Hard to Find* by **Aaron Fagan**

36. *Rough Song* by **Blanca Varela**

37. *In the Same Light: Poems For Our Century From the Migrants & Exiles of the Tang Dynasty, translations* by **Wong May**

38. *On the Mesa: An Anthology of Bolinas Writing (50th Anniversary Edition), edited by* **Ben Estes and Joel Weishaus**

39. *Listen My Friend, This Is the Dream I Dreamed Last Night* by **Cody-Rose Clevidence**